- Renew books by phoning 01305 224311 or online www.dorsetforyou.com/libraries

- Items may be returned to any Dorset library.

- Please note that children's books issued on an adult card will incur overdue charges.

Dorset County Council
Library Service

DL/2372 dd05450

7/unc

LAST DAYS OF STEAM
SOUTHERN REGION

A PERSONAL PHOTOGRAPHIC MEMOIR

ROGER MALONE

HALSGROVE

First published in Great Britain in 2008

British Library Cataloguing-in-Publication Data
A CIP record for this title is available from the British Library

ISBN 978 1 84114 754 3

HALSGROVE
Halsgrove House,
Ryelands Industrial Estate,
Bagley Road, Wellington, Somerset TA21 9PZ
Tel: 01823 653777 Fax: 01823 216796
email: sales@halsgrove.com
website: www.halsgrove.com

Printed and bound by Grafiche Flaminia, Italy

INTRODUCTION

This collection of images comes from almost a lifetime away. Yet the memories are as fresh as yesterday. There was that youthful awe and wonder at a locomotive's huge presence, simmering impatiently at the platform's edge; the hiss of steam, warmth from the boiler and that addictive aroma of the engine's hot breath. All that pent-up energy then unleashed in a percussive display of power as it inched its load away from the station.

While the distancing decades have blurred much detail from those teenage years, the magic of steam remains as evocative now as it did then.

The pictures and notes taken at the time have served well in reinforcing my recall, providing a time-travel ticket to the past.

My enduring enthusiasm was fired with the inevitable clockwork train set, an essential rite of passage for any child of the fifties. Living in Plymouth, there were constant appeals to my father to park the car for a spot of train watching every time we were in the vicinity of the station, which was then served by both the Southern Region and Western Region. I remember nothing from those infant visits except salient colours. Bright green coaches. Carmine and cream coaches. Black engines. Dark green engines. And billowing plumes of white smoke.

At home I felt compelled to draw them, colouring in the naively executed shapes with crayons. Was that when the seeds were sown for worshipping at the shrine of the Southern? I wish some of those pictures still existed. How many coaches did I colour green? They could have provided an intriguing insight into the origins of a life-time's fascination with steam in general, the Southern in particular and a desire to somehow distill it through images.

A number of years on, I was given a copy of The Observer's Book of Railway Locomotives of Britain. This detailed all the classes and where they were located. It immediately gave some structure and insight into a hobby that hitherto, while enjoyed, was little understood.

I thumbed the pages so frequently that, while not setting out to, I grew to absorb the names and numbers of favourite classes as if by osmosis. Sadly a technique not so diligently achieved when it came to school work!

The downside was that dieselisation had advanced at such a rate much information gleaned from the pages had been rapidly overtaken by events.

Steam locomotives were, by the early 60s, being withdrawn with escalating haste. Many pre-grouping classes, those built before 1922, when the myriad smaller railway companies were amalgamated into the Big Four (the GWR, LMS, LNER and SR), were by now extinct. Those classes remaining had their days numbered in the headlong rush towards modernisation.

By the time I acquired the book, steam in Devon was virtually extinct. But it proved a vital catalyst. Things were clearly not going to remain the same, and now, as an enthusiastic young photographer, I became keen to capture whatever I could on camera.

The fact I had been using transparency film since I was about 12, in an era when most took colour prints or black and white, was a huge stroke of good fortune.

I owe that to an inspirational slide show staged by a friend of the family. As the lights went out and the projector went on, one large illuminated image after another dazzled the screen. Possessing so much more impact that the printed alternative, here was a modern day magic lantern show, and I was hooked.

All interest in print film was eclipsed by an allegiance to transparencies which has lasted well into the digital age. By the time, in the mid 60s, I went on my first 'steam sortie', I was using a 35mm camera loaded with 36-exposure Kodachrome film.

It was now 1965. Save for a seemingly forgotten "USA" tank at Meldon Quarry on the windswept edge of Dartmoor, and a welcome trickle of steam enthusiast specials utilising locomotives based elsewhere, Devon and Cornwall was devoid of steam. By this point, the nearest place to Plymouth to see regular mainline steam in action was Weymouth. It was, like all steam routes, on borrowed time.

My second stroke of good fortune, after discovering the delights of transparencies, was in having a father who, despite no deep interest in railways himself, was generous enough with his time to help me pursue my fascination with the subject.

A regular subscriber to railway magazines now, I was, at last, clued up to the current railway scene, not trailing several years behind due to obsolete literature! And it was then, I realised how near the end of the line steam now was.

I persuaded my parents a day by the Dorset seaside could be healthy for them – and a day by the lineside would be hugely beneficial for me.

And so, courtesy of their willingness to sample the joys of Weymouth, we bundled into the faithful old blue Ford Cortina for what was to be the first of many jaunts to the Jurassic Coast by car.

Such outings were always a delight. Not only was there the anticipation of steam, but the enchanting coastal run along the Bridport-Abbotsbury road, with its sweeping views of Chesil Beach curving towards Portland Bill, to savour as well.

Weymouth beguiled me from my first visit. Here, for the steam starved, were sulphurous riches beyond one's wildest dreams.

We all have our preferences for whatever reasons, and the Southern has always been mine. In simplistic terms I think it was the appeal of green coaches, so evocative of rural byways recalled from early childhood trips to parts of Devon that were, in those days, undiluted Southern territory. And then there was the eponymous West Country Class Pacifics, a type of locomotive wedded by name to the very region it served.

These Bulleid Light Pacifics (called 'light' to differentiate from their heavier cousins, the Merchant Navy Pacifics) have always been my firm favourites. A class divided into West Country and Battle of Britain Pacifics, they were identical in all but name. They possessed nice touches of eye-catching individuality ensuring they had that unmistakable Bulleid "signature". There was the oval smokebox doors, and striking wheels, and, in their un-rebuilt state, which some of the class retained throughout their life, a revolutionary "air-smoothed" casing.

Weymouth offered a Southern Region version of a hazily recalled Dawlish outing viewed as a five-year-old in the 50s. Then the Western Region bedazzled young eyes with a seemingly ceaseless cavalcade of Torbay and Cornish Riviera-bound summer Saturday excursions.

Fast forward a decade and, now a 15 year old in the mid-60s, I was able to savour every magical moment of a Southern equivalent with Channel Islands boat trains and expresses bound for Bournemouth and beyond.

With just two years of Souther Region steam left to run I resolved to record what I could. However a pocket-money purchased roll of Kodachrome 36-exposure film had to be used relatively sparingly despite the tempting array of subject matter.

With hindsight I wish I had taken more pictures, but in truth I'm more than grateful I was fortunate enough to record as much as I did. Compared with older photographers who started earlier, the amount may be humble and the content less diverse. But because of what these transparencies record, they are my most prized railway images.

Without them, and now some 40 years on, it would have all seemed an unlikely dream. As it is it becomes harder and harder to believe I was a youthful observer on the sidelines, when these snorting steam dinosaurs were once part of the everyday transport scene. A far cry, indeed, from today's preened celebrities of preservation.

It is an irony that in the post 1980s era of preserved mainline steam I might devote one film and a whole day happily chasing a single enthusiasts' special; while in the 60s one film would not have had enough exposures to capture every locomotive seen on a busy summer Saturday.

Despite the splendid sight and sound of 21st century mainline steam stoking memories of past glories, it is no substitute for what I call 'real steam'. I look back on that with a huge well of warmth and nostalgia – an emotion that ensnares us all at certain ages, and one, I am sure, shared equally by diesel enthusiasts addicted to their own decades of remembered glories.

I confess to a slight grain of truth when I wryly tell people the only thing that stops me wishing I was younger is the fact I would have missed the Indian Summer of British Railways' shrinking steam fleet!

From 1965 to the end of Southern steam in 1967, and the extinction of British Railways' final pocket of steam corralled in the Lancashire area of the Midland Region in 1968, I saw as much and more as any teenage schoolboy – dependent on pocket money, subsidised transport and parental goodwill – could reasonably hope for.

There was a sizeable list of locomotive depots that followed, including Carlisle Kingmoor – in 1967 the largest allocation of steam locomotives in the country. But Weymouth was the first major fully operational steam shed I ever walked into. It was appropriately Southern, and simmering with an abundance of steam.

Weymouth locomotive depot was originally built by the Great Western Railway. When it opened in 1857, the line was shared jointly between the GWR and the London and South Western Railway from Weymouth to Dorchester, where the companies then went their separate ways. However, after the railways were nationalised in

1948, it was transferred to the Southern Region.

To be able to wander about this stable, dominated by Bulleid-designed thoroughbreds, the Merchant Navy, West Country and Battle of Britain Class Pacifics; to step out of the sunlight into that dark lair of a shed where the senses were assailed by looming metallic shapes and the smell and sound of gently escaping steam, was an amazing experience.

Unlike some sheds, the staff were pleasantly tolerant of enthusiasts, and I found a polite request to look around was never refused. Maybe in this dying era of steam they were perhaps glad that the twilight of their anthracite-eating charges was being chronicled by anyone, even someone as insignificant as a teenager clutching a camera. Or maybe, at this late stage in the game, they were disillusioned and really didn't care. I like to think it was the former.

So many sheds at the end of steam were redundant, and either converted to some other use or demolished. Weymouth ultimately became a housing estate.

For me two other special locations ranked side by side with Weymouth as places I was particularly keen to visit.

One was the Somerset and Dorset Joint Railway and the other the Isle of Wight. The former was to experience, albeit in its final gasp, something of the essence of this celebrated, fiercely graded route over the Mendips from Bath to Bournemouth. The latter was to see the last outpost of the former LSWR O2 Class 0-4-4 tank engines.

It should not have been possible to visit the Somerset and Dorset when I did. It should have already been closed.

The sad demise of the S and D (dubbed 'slow and dirty' or 'swift and delightful' depending on a passenger's particular point of view!) was a painful, prolonged affair. The line was owned jointly by the Southern Railway and London Midland and Scottish Railway prior to nationalisation, when it became part of the Southern Region in 1948. The fate of this undulating route was sealed when the section between Bath and Templecombe came under the control of the Western Region in 1958. Gradually through trains, including the Pines Express linking the North West and the South Coast, either disappeared or were re-routed away from the S and D. The line was systematically downgraded until only local services survived.

This calculated demolition job caused a deliberate and unstoppable downward spiral in the line's fortunes and made it a perfect candidate for closure. Apart from being, in its heyday, a much in demand cross country rail corridor to the coast, the Somerset and Dorset was an absolute Mecca for railway enthusiasts.

It's attractions were many: it remained totally steam operated to the end; it had challenging gradients often requiring double-heading on heavy trains, and an eclectic array of locomotives including its very own impressive 7F Class 2-8-0.

My visit was seven weeks after it was due to close – and two before it did. Fortunately, a bus company, which was to operate an alternative service pulled out, providing a brief reprieve for the S and D. It was a bleak half term Monday in February 1966 when I stepped off the Warship Class diesel hydraulic-hauled 10.25 Exeter-Waterloo service. Templecombe was where the former Southern Railway's West of England mainline between Salisbury and Exeter connected with, and crossed over, the S and D.

There was just time for a soup-and-sandwich snack in the station cafe before BR Standard Class 4 2-6-4T No 80013 rumbled past to retrieve coaches from the yard. It then propelled them back to the S and D platform. Shortly after, an ex-LMS 2MT Ivatt 2-6-2T came up from the motive power depot and coupled on to the rear. It drew the

12.30 Bournemouth-bound service down the connecting spur to the S and D and uncoupled, releasing the train to journey south, before returning to the depot.

This fascinating ritual happened for all Bournemouth-bound trains, while for those arriving from Bournemouth, a locomotive was similarly attached to the rear to draw the reversing train up the gradient to Templecombe station. The shed had 10 locomotives, three in steam. One, Standard Class 4 No 80043, was to head the 2pm to Bath which I was soon to board.

Here, for me, began a 36-mile journey into railway legend. There was the stiff, mainly 1 in 50, ascent of the Mendips to the summit at Masbury, and names like Evercreech Junction which echoed with the ghosts of summer Saturdays when double-headed trains pounded their way north to Bath.

Another such railway legend was the Isle of Wight. Like some strange steam reservation, here, embraced by the Solent, was the last concentration of ex-LSWR O2 0-4-2Ts. Long since disappeared from the mainland, these delightful, vintage locomotives were in sole charge of this fascinating and, by now, vastly truncated system.

The Isle of Wight was an enchanting, sun-drenched time warp with O2s bustling about, shuttling suitcase-clutching holidaymakers between Ryde Pier and Shanklin. There was a certain appeal in the ubiquitousness of this pleasantly-proportioned class of locomotive, rattling along with its antique green coaches. Yet this was the last summer of such a constant aspect of island life. Soon the lines would hum to the strains of former London Transport underground stock. Perhaps some things didn't change. The Isle of Wight railway was once again the recipient of items redundant from elsewhere.

After the end of Southern steam, there was still an intriguing location featuring working steam to be found deep in Hampshire at the Longmoor Military Railway.

This was built by the Royal Engineers from 1903 to train soldiers in the skills of railway construction and operation. Connected to the BR network at Liss, at its peak, it ran to 70 miles of operational laid track and sidings. As a training railway, parts were often constructed and de-constructed and bits of the layout would sometimes be changed – a bit like a giant train set!

I managed two visits in 1968. The first to see wildlife artist and railway enthusiast David Shepherd's 9F Class 2-10-0 No 92203 officially named 'Black Prince', and the second to visit an open day which featured a number of the LMR's locomotives including immaculate blue-liveried standard Austerity 2-10-0 'Gordon' and 0-6-0ST 'Errol Lonsdale'.

The railway closed down a year later. Enthusiasts tried to buy the small, but complete system, but the MOD was only prepared to sell a one-and-a-half mile section at Liss. Local residents blocked that by purchasing a section of land, scuppering a unique opportunity for preservationists.

With the end of BR steam now a painful reality, preserved railways offered some consolation with their neatly sanitised re-creation of a grime-encrusted past.

But it was to South Wales and Woodham Brothers' scrapyard at Barry that disciples of steam were drawn in droves to mourn their dear departed and pay their last respects.

My first of several visits was in 1966 on an enthusiasts' outing from Plymouth. It conveyed the faithful to this vast graveyard of decaying locomotives, bronzed by the rust-inducing salt-sea air blowing up the Bristol Channel.

Here dinosaurs of the steam age passively awaited the coup de grace of the cutter's torch.

But for many, this steam cemetery was to be their salvation. While other scrapyards quickly cut up their charges, Woodham Brothers had a sufficient reserve of work to keep the locomotives on the back burner. As a result an amazing number were ultimately saved by preservationists who raised enough cash to buy these hulks and painstakingly bring them back from the dead. So, decades later, locomotives whose fires were dropped in the dying embers of BR steam, rose again, rescued, restored and resplendently glinting in a new era.

Mainline steam had come back, polished to perfection, capturing the spirit of the old days, not only to the delight of railway enthusiasts that remembered them, but also a new audience too young to have experienced it first time around. But for me, however enjoyable steam is in the 21st century, it cannot beat the old days. And, in true nostalgic tradition, when I reflect on them, it is the sunny times I recall with most affection.

If I had to pick a favourite, I think it would be the day spent in the chalk hills south of Dorchester. Here, the line rose steadily to Bincombe Tunnel before dropping steeply all the way to Weymouth. I remember a liberating sense of space and wide skies. A glorious summer's day with non-stop sun, and a breeze gently swaying the long grasses that carpeted the lineside. Here was seemingly timeless tranquility. Long, languid periods of silence interrupted only by the percussive beat of passing locomotives and occasional drone of nectar-seeking bees. I can still feel that sunshine.

BARRY

This page and opposite: Wagon wheels keep the cutter's torch busy – giving the locomotives longer to be saved.

Hope on the horizon as preservationists stake their claims on the rust-clad objects of their affection. Not all locomotives survived – but a lot did. Between 1959 and 1968 almost 300 locomotives had been bought by Woodhams, and 213 were eventually saved.

A BR Class 9F 2-10-0 awaits its fate as nature starts to claw its way through the rust. This class of locomotive made occasional inroads into Southern territory and, for a while, hauled heavy summer expresses on the Somerset and Dorset.

A sea of turquoise drums lap around the hulk of former SECR U Class 2-6-0 No 31625, making a surreal study.

Pillaged for every useable part, despite the painted plea on the side, this streamlined SR Battle of Britain Class Pacific suffers from the final ignominy of being paired with an ex-GWR tender! While their designer, OVS Bulleid, referred to their streamlined state as 'air-smoothed casing' they quickly acquired the nickname 'spam cans'. This affectionate tag was possibly because the Pacifics were introduced at a time in the 1940s when spam (luncheon meat imported from the States as part of the war effort) was very much on the menu. A wry comparison was drawn between the shape of the air-smoothed Bulleid… and a spam can!

On misty days the scrapyard took on a brooding atmosphere as locomotive shapes in various states of decay and destruction played Russian roulette with the cutter's torch.

Marooned in rows of dead engines – Merchant Navy Pacific No 35011, General Steam Navigation, stands stripped of its former glory. Fortunately it, together with a further ten members of the class, is still with us today.

The tide of scrap at Woodham Brothers, Barry, South Glamorgan, had receded as steam engines were rescued, leaving this BR Standard Class locomotive stranded in a rising sea of brambles.

Salvation for many... Steam engines can be glimpsed beyond an abundance of wagon wheels. The acquisition of condemned wagons, withdrawn in BR's headlong rush towards modernisation, provided sufficient work to keep the scrapping of locomotives to a minimum.

LONGMOOR
MILITARY
RAILWAY

This page and opposite: Wildlife artist and railway enthusiast David Shepherd purchased former BR Standard 9F Class 2-10-0 No 92203. He had it officially named *Black Prince* at a ceremony well-attended by both the public and media at the Longmoor Military Railway in Hampshire. The event took place after the immaculate locomotive drew its train into Longmoor Downs station from the junction with BR at Liss. Apart from green-liveried *Evening Star*, the last steam engine built by British Railways in 1960, all members of the class spent their working lives in unlined black, and none carried names. The 9Fs bizarrely gained the nickname 'spaceships'. Apparently, the big gap between boiler and footplate made the boiler appear a dead ringer for the booster stages used in the 60s NASA space project. Swinging sixties and steam driven rockets – how psychedelic was that? 8 June 1968.

This page and opposite: Austerity 0-6-0 saddle tank Errol Lonsdale takes on coal before preparing to leave Longmoor Downs station with a passenger train on the Longmoor Military Railway Open Day. A year later the MOD-run railway was closed. Gordon now resides on the Severn Valley Railway and Errol Lonsdale is on the South Devon Railway. 28 September 1968.

It is Open Day at Longmoor Military Railway as Standard Austerity Class 2-10-0 *Gordon* draws its train towards Longmoor Downs. This system was built by the Royal Engineers to train soldiers in railway construction and operation. The standard livery of LMR locomotives was a smart royal blue lined in red, with red rods and yellow lettering. The stock next to *Gordon* is a very elderly ex-London Brighton and South Coast Railway 'birdcage' passenger brake coach. 28 September 1968.

LAUNCESTON

Ex-LMS 2MT Ivatt 2-6-2 tank locomotive No 41283 coasts towards Lydford on the former Southern Railway main line between Exeter and Plymouth. Organised by the Great Western Society, the special was celebrating the Launceston branch centenary and was the last steam train to Cornwall. 5 September 1965.

No 41283 has arrived at Lydford station, which was shared by the SR and GWR. Having crossed over from the Southern lines and run around its coaches, it prepares to travel bunker-first along the former GWR branch to Launceston. Note the GWR water tower and lower quadrant signal. 5 September 1965.

The passage of the special through Lifton caused considerable interest among the locals. The guard protected the progress of the train as it eased over the level crossing. 5 September 1965.

Having approached Launceston along the GWR branch line, which originated in Plymouth, the Ivatt 2-6-2T has drawn its train into the town's former Southern Railway station. While the locomotive takes water, the passengers have a chance to stretch their legs. The signal box can be seen on the up platform. 5 September 1965.

With a good head of steam Ivatt 2-6-2T No 41283 now heads its train away from Launceston on the remainder of the trip, which took it back to Exeter via Okehampton. 5 September 1965.

MELDON

DS234 shunts trucks with the quarry face rising dramatically in the background. Originally worked as a small quarry for local railway requirements in 1874, it was, in 1879, developed to provide most of the LSWR ballast. September 1965.

Passing the single locomotive shed at Meldon, the 'USA' 0-6-0T draws its completed train towards the main line for collection. Designed by the US Army Transportation Corps in 1942 for heavy duty dock shunting, 14 were purchased by the Southern Railway in 1946. Quite un-English in appearance, they were typical American 'switcher', or shunting engines, with stove-pipe chimneys and three domes. September 1965.

Under the watchful eye of the shunter the locomotive approaches the main line. Ahead can be seen the short platforms which were once used for quarry staff. Beyond, is the graceful, girdered Meldon Viaduct built in 1874. The ballast train was taken away by a Hymek diesel-hydraulic bound for Exeter. September 1965.

The day's work is done. DS234 retires to its shed, and the shunter kindly poses for a photograph beside the locomotive. September 1965.

The end of the line for 'USA' Class 0-6-0T DS234, formerly No 30062. It is a splendid, small victory that this locomotive survived, seemingly forgotten, in this wind-swept moorland outpost long after mainline steam had been ousted west of Yeovil. Finally, replaced by a diesel shunter, the last BR steam engine working in Devon awaits its fate. 19 November 1966.

ISLE OF WIGHT RAILWAY

Two ex-London and South Western Railway O2 Class 0-4-4Ts meet at Sandown. I have a particular affection for this picture because it conveys so much of the atmosphere of the era. The platform is bustling with passengers and suitcases; at the platform's edge is the paraphernalia of lineside signs and signals; even the trees and cotton-wool clouds play their supporting role in this seemingly timeless Southern scene. 18 June 1966.

The motive power depot was right alongside Ryde St John's Road Station. Being a busy summer Saturday the shed area was sparsely populated, with just one O2 being prepared for duty. The attractive 45-lever signalbox, in Southern colours of green and cream, was formerly located at Waterloo East. It was brought over from the mainland in the 1920s. 18 June 1966.

For some locomotives their passenger duty days were already done. Their fires dropped for the last time and shunted into a siding are No 21 *Sandown*, No 29 *Alverstone* and No 26 *Whitwell*. 18 June 1966.

At Shanklin, now the end of the line since the section to Ventnor closed in April 1966, an O2 arrives with its train. 18 June 1966.

Having run around its coaches at Shanklin, No 31 *Chale* departs, bunker first, for the return trip to Ryde Pier. 18 June 1966.

This page and opposite: All the O2s were named after places on the island. Here No 33 *Bembridge* heads along Ryde Pier with the Solent's blue waters to its side, and arrives at the terminus with its ferry connection to the mainland. 18 June 1966.

A broadside of *Bembridge*, displaying the attractive lines of this ex-LSWR Class locomotive, which was introduced in 1889. Fitted with Westinghouse brakes that made a distinctive rhythmic panting noise, the pumps can be seen on the left hand side of the smokebox. Once regular sights on West Country branchlines, the Isle of Wight O2s had outlived their mainland brethren and, in their last summer, were a magnet for enthusiasts. 18 June 1966.

SOMERSET & DORSET

This page and opposite: The rain has cleared, and the platform shines after the recent downpour as BR Standard Class 4 2-6-4T No 80013 stands at Templecombe Station with the 12.30 stopping train for Bournemouth. 21 February 1966.

As the black clouds recede, No 80013 – with an obscured Ivatt 2MT 2-6-2T piloting the train at the rear – catches a burst of sunlight as it descends the spur from Templecombe to the metals of the former Somerset and Dorset Joint Railway. 21 February 1966.

Having reversed down the connecting spur, visible in the background, and been uncoupled from the pilot engine at the junction, No 80013 now heads purposefully towards Bournemouth. It will shortly pass under the Southern's West of England main line just east of Templecombe station. 21 February 1966.

Templecombe motive power depot with BR Standard Class 4 2-6-4T No 80043 wreathed in steam. 21 February 1966.

Pictured from the 14.00 departure for Bath, as it descended to join the S and D, is Ivatt 2MT 2-6-2T No 41249 beside the shed. In the background is sister locomotive No 41283. 21 February 1966.

In light steam outside Templecombe shed is BR Standard Class 4 2-6-0 No 76011. I would later pass this locomotive on a passenger train near Binegar during my return journey to Templecombe. 21 February 1966.

Bathed in low February sunlight, BR Standard Class 4 2-6-0 No 76014, minus it number plate, simmers at the elegant canopied terminus of Bath Green Park, prior to departing with the 16.25 for Templecombe. The positioning of the two lamps on the smokebox form a standard headcode displayed on all trains on the S and D. 21 February 1966.

Opposite page, left: Snapped on the approach lines at Bath Junction, was ex-GWR pannier tank No 3681. 21 February 1966.

Opposite page, right: En route through the undulating landscape of the Somerset and Dorset behind Standard Class 4 2-6-4T No 80043. The route was born in 1862, through the amalgamation of the Somerset Central Railway and the Dorset Central Railway. 21 February 1966.

Ex-London Midland and Scottish Railway 'Jinty' 0-6-0T No 47276 was shunting wagons at Braysdown Colliery sidings near Writhlington Signal Box, just past Radstock. On a line now operated primarily by BR Standard Class locomotives, I felt it quite a coup glimpsing this engine at work, likewise ex-Great Western Railway 0-6-0 pannier tank No 3681 working the sidings at Bath. In its heyday the Somerset and Dorset was host to SR, LMS and GWR locomotives, as well as being home to its very own SDJR Class 7F 2-8-0 freight locomotives. It is an irony, in this era of increasing rarities, that 'Jinty' and GWR pannier tanks once ranked amongst the most common classes of locomotives in their respective regions! 21 February 1966.

I have included this because Evercreech Junction was an important station in the foothills of the Mendips in those distant days when the line bustled with cross-country holiday traffic. On summer Saturdays, the centre siding would be packed with locomotives waiting to pilot north-bound expresses over the stiff Mendips gradients to Bath. From here, trains faced an eight-mile slog at predominantly 1 in 50 to the summit at Masbury. As our train took water, the ghosts of those past glories still reverberated through the decaying silence of a station soon to be laid to rest. 21 February 1966.

BOURNEMOUTH

It is mid-afternoon and Merchant Navy Class Pacific No 35007 *Aberdeen Commonwealth* has arrived with the 'Bournemouth Belle' Pullman from Waterloo. This prestigious service lasted no longer than steam with the final train operating on Sunday, 9 July, 1967. 29 October 1966.

West Country Pacific No 34104 *Bere Alston* starts a Waterloo express from Bournemouth after a bout of wheel slipping, something these locomotives were prone to. Built at Eastleigh in 1950 it was the last Pacific to shed its 'air smoothed' casing and be rebuilt in 1961. 29 October 1966.

Battle of Britain Class Pacific No 34088 *213 Squadron* eases into Bournemouth Central. A relative, knowing I had travelled to Bournemouth, asked if I enjoyed the beach. I had to admit to never venturing beyond the station boundaries. That sounded quite sad, I suppose. But, at the time, I was very single-minded where steam was concerned. In post-steam, post-teenage life, I have sampled the beach at Bournemouth on a number of occasions. And very nice it is too. 29 October 1966.

BR Standard Class 4 No 76026 approaches from the west, passing Bournemouth locomotive depot. The coal trucks were an essential part of the shed scene. Just visible are the chimneys of two Ivatt 2MT tanks. 29 October 1966.

Slowly getting into its stride No 34088 *213 Squadron* pulls away from the long down platform at Bournemouth. 29 October 1966.

A Weymouth-Waterloo express arrives at Bournemouth behind Merchant Navy Class Pacific No 35014 *Nederland Line*. Although in externally poor condition, it still retained its nameplates and smokebox number plate at a time when many Bulleid Pacifics were nameless and even numberless. The two centre tracks that ran through the station had just been lifted and work was going on in preparation for electrification of the line. 10 December 1966.

The low sun highlights the wheel and high running board of BR Standard Class 4 2-6-0 No 76011 in this broadside of it on Bournemouth motive power depot's turntable, behind the up platform. 10 December 1966.

Just up from Weymouth, BR Standard Class 4 No 76026 takes water at Bournemouth before continuing its journey. 29 October 1966.

What a bonus to find such a pristine West Country at Bournemouth motive power depot! With nothing to detract from its sun-drenched good looks No 34047 *Callington* makes a fine picture as it is being prepared for its next duty. 29 October 1966.

Just arrived at Bournemouth, the 11.18 from Weymouth, which I had travelled on. Under the dirt of this BR Standard Class 5 4-6-0 No 73029 is a lined green livery. 10 December 1966.

Begrimed West Country Pacific No 34018 *Axminster* arrives from Weymouth. It survived to the end of steam, being withdrawn in July, 1967, with a final mileage of 974,317. 29 October 1966.

Standards on parade at Bournemouth motive power depot. 10 December 1966.

EASTLEIGH

The Flying Scotsman has arrived at Eastleigh with a railway enthusiasts' special which was then to travel on to Salisbury with a pair of BR Standard Class 4 2-6-4T locomotives. Here, the preserved ex-London and North Eastern Railway Pacific shunts forward prior to reversing through the station to the sheds. Note the crowds lining the platform, and the trespassing photographers of which, I am now ashamed to admit, I was one! In my defence, I merely copied others who should have known better... But then, so should I. 17 September 1966.

The centre of attention. I wish now I paid more attention to the anonymous Ivatt 2MT tank in the background. *The Flying Scotsman* is still here today basking in celebrity status. Sadly, the humble Ivatt is not. 17 September 1966.

A tale of two Pacifics – to the left, Merchant Navy Pacific No 35017 *Belgian Marine*, its glory days over; to the right *The Flying Scotsman*, probably the world's most famous steam locomotive. 17 September 1966.

There was an air of excitement amongst onlookers as the 'Bournemouth Belle' thundered through Eastleigh on its way to the coast behind Merchant Navy Pacific *Lamport & Holt Line*. 17 September 1966.

Whenever I have projected this image I have called it 'Speed'! It usually got a laugh; truth is the shutter wasn't fast enough for the job. But I still like it. Somehow, by default, it conveys much of the sheer might and muscle of a Bulleid Pacific at full throttle. Sometimes, a perfect picture can be too perfect and an imperfect one can actually say more. But then, I would say that. 17 September 1966.

Don't you just love the young trio of train spotters in sandals, socks, shorts and matching shirts concentrating on the action? Here BR Standard Class 5 4-6-0 No 73022 simmers at Eastleigh while West Country Pacific No 34093 *Saunton* thunders through on a down express. 17 September 1966.

West Country Pacific *Callington* speeds its Waterloo-bound passengers along the up through line at Eastleigh. 17 September 1966.

A brace of BR Standard Class 4 2-6-4Ts. No 80152 piloting No 80016, prepares to depart from Eastleigh with an enthusiasts' round trip to Salisbury. 17 September 1966.

Always a delight to behold was a member of the much diminished number of un-rebuilt Bulleid Light Pacifics still in service. Here, No 34006 *Bude* ambles past with an engineers' train at Eastleigh. This locomotive took part in the 1948 Locomotive Exchanges and was unique in its class for having the longest smoke deflectors. 17 September 1966.

AROUND EXETER

A very rare visitor. Ex-LNER A2 Pacific No 60532 *Blue Peter*, more familiar with the Scottish main line between Glasgow and Edinburgh than the Southern, arrives at Exeter Central with a Locomotive Club of Great Britain railtour. The sole survivor of the A2 Class, and at the time allocated to Dundee, *Blue Peter* was much in demand for railtours. It was withdrawn from service at the end of 1966 and purchased for preservation in 1968. With the help of the BBC children's programme of the same name, it was restored to working condition once more. 14 August 1966.

Blue Peter pulls forward into the carriage sidings at the west end of Exeter Central prior to reversing back to the station, watched by a crowd of admirers. 14 August 1966.

Before boundary changes gave operational powers to the Western Region, and steam was withdrawn from the West Country, Exmouth Junction was the most important SR motive power depot west of Salisbury. It was a major player with a large number of locomotives on its books. Now, in the autumn of 1965 all that could be found were two ex-GWR 0-6-0 pannier tanks in BR lined green livery beneath the grime. Their BR days done, ex GWR 64XX Class 0-6-0PTs No 6412 and 6430 had been set aside for preservation. Late 1965.

Although no longer having a steam allocation in late 1965, Exmouth Junction motive power depot did occasionally play host to visiting locomotives such as these two BR Standard Class 4 2-6-4Ts, No 80039 and No 80043. Both locomotives were based at Templecombe and had travelled to Exeter to haul a railtour to North Devon the following day. 2 October 1965.

Un-rebuilt West Country Pacific No 34006 *Bude* arrives at Sidmouth Junction with an enthusiasts' special that was to be hauled along the branch by a waiting Hymek diesel-hydraulic. The un-rebuilt locomotives were very different from the rebuilt members of the class, except for the elliptical smoke box door, 'solid' box pox wheels and tender with its slightly tapered base. 2 April 1966.

Having drawn its train partly ahead of the down platform, and blocking the level crossing (immediately this side of the footbridge), *Bude* prepares to uncouple from its coaches. It then runs light to Exmouth Junction for turning and servicing. Carriage doors are open and enthusiasts walk along the lineside to take pictures. Something that would not be tolerated under today's health and safety edicts! 2 April 1966.

Coaled, watered and turned at Exmouth Junction, West Country No 34006 *Bude* has returned to Sidmouth Junction to collect its train. Here, it makes a splendid sight departing on the homeward run. Sidmouth Junction closed in 1967 with the cessation of passenger services to Sidmouth, and to Exmouth via Tipton St Johns. However, due to a resurgence of custom on the line, it reopened in 1971 under its original name of Feniton. 2 April 1966.

Merchant Navy Class Pacific No 35023 *Holland-Afrika Line*, minus nameplates, drifts into Exeter Central with an enthusiasts' special from Waterloo. Although originally owned by the London and South Western Railway, absorbed by the Southern Railway and, after nationalisation, operated by the Southern Region, the line to Salisbury was transferred to the Western Region in 1963. 26 June 1966.

Having left Exeter behind No 35023 *Holland-Afrika* Line is seen at Cowley Bridge Junction. The line was shared between the SR and WR from Exeter St David's to here, where it split, with the former Southern route veering west towards Plymouth and the Atlantic Coast, and the Western Region line curving east. Having left Southern metals at Exeter Central, and descended the incline to St David's, No 35023 is returning to Waterloo via Taunton, Westbury and Salisbury. 26 June 1966.

Un-rebuilt West Country Class Pacific No 34015 *Exmouth* prepares to depart from Exeter Central. Unlike most locomotive classes that used lamps to denote headcodes, Bulleid Pacifics had electric lights powered by a steam generator to reinforce the position of the white discs in the dark. The discs, on the Southern, were used to denote which route a train was taking. On other regions lamp codes generally related to the type of train. 8 January 1966.

No 35026 *Lamport & Holt* Line gets admiring looks at Exeter Central, which was originally known as Exeter Queen Street. 15 October 1966.

The 1 in 37 gradient from Exeter St David's up to Exeter Central is a stiff climb. In a spectacular display of sound and steam Merchant Navy Class Pacific No 35026 *Lamport & Holt Line* arrives with a railtour that has reached Exeter via the Western Region main line and will travel back to London via the former Southern route to the capital. The Merchant Navies, which handled crack expresses from Waterloo to the West of England, never normally went beyond Exeter Central because of weight restrictions. Such duties were left in the capable hands of the Bulleid Light Pacifics, the West Country and Battle of Britain Classes. 15 October 1966.

One welcome break in the clouds allowed the sun to highlight No 35026 *Lamport & Holt Line* as it drew its coaches forward before setting them back into a bay platform. There were 30 members of this class, introduced in 1941 with streamlined casing to the design of the chief mechanical engineer of the Southern Railway, OVS Bulleid, and all rebuilt in the late 50s. 15 October 1966.

Time to go. No 35026 *Lamport & Holt* Line eases its train away from Exeter Central. It's interesting to note the new position of the white discs. On the Western Region their position denoted the type of train; for the journey on the former Southern Railway they have been altered to act as route indicators. The one above, the other below the smokebox signifies a train running on the SR West of England main line. 15 October 1966.

DORSET

Battle of Britain Pacific No 34089 *602 Squadron* heads along the single track of the Swanage branch between Corfe Castle and the seaside terminus. A BR Standard Class 4 2-6-4T was attached to the rear for the return journey. 18 June 1967.

Viewed from the vantage point of Corfe Castle the Swanage line looks a little like a model railway. Here BR Standard Class 4 2-6-4T No 80146 leads the train back to Wareham with Battle of Britain Class Pacific No 34089 *602 Squadron* trailing. 18 June 1967.

Battle of Britain Class Pacific *602 Squadron* trails, as the special heads back along the Swanage branch towards Wareham. 18 June 1967

Sun and shade. A perfect spot to watch the approach of Battle of Britain Class Pacific No 34089 *602 Squadron* speeding west on the Dorchester side of Wareham. 18 June 1967.

A pair of ex-LMS 2MT Ivatt 2-6-2 tanks arrive at Maiden Newton station on the former GWR route from Castle Cary to Weymouth prior to taking a railtour along the Bridport branch. They were affectionately known as 'Mickey Mouse' tanks because of their shape, front end-on. 22 January 1967.

The special arrives behind smartly turned out West Country Pacific No 34013 *Okehampton* which was rebuilt in 1957. A lot of this class were officially named by civic dignitaries in the stations of the towns they were named after. 22 January 1967.

Just time for enthusiasts to photograph No 34013 *Okehampton* before it departs, light engine, to Weymouth. 22 January 1967.

Left: Passing at Poole. Weymouth-bound West Country Pacific No 34036 *Westward Ho* eases into the station. No exclamation marks on the locomotive – even if there is one on the resort named after the book written by Charles Kingsley in the mid 1800s! 29 October 1966.

Below: BR Standard Class 5 No 73119 awaits its departure time in the sun at Portsmouth. 18 June 1966.

Right: October sun gilds the 15.23 Bournemouth – Weymouth train as it heads along the causeway near Parkstone with rebuilt West Country No 34001 *Exeter* at the helm. Built in 1945 at Brighton as an "air smoothed" locomotive, Exeter, then given the Southern Railway number of 21C101, was the first of what was to be 110 members of the West Country/Battle of Britain Class Bulleid Pacifics. 29 October 1966.

Above: A BR Standard Class 4 2-6-0 drifts down the 1 in 91 bank from Bincombe Tunnel towards Dorchester. 10 June 1967.

A perfect afternoon as BR Standard Class 4 2-6-0 hauls a short train up towards Bincombe Tunnel from Weymouth. 10 June 1967.

About a mile south of Dorchester is the abandoned Monkton and Came Halt, opened in 1905 and closed in 1957. Here, travelling 'light engine' to the coast, is West Country Pacific No 34100 *Appledore*. 10 June 1967.

BR Standard Class 4 2-6-0 No 76007 climbs away from Dorchester on the last leg of its journey to the coast. 10 June 1967.

95

It is just after noon and Merchant Navy Pacific No 35008 *Orient Line*, with a Waterloo-Weymouth boat train, takes the steady climb to Bincombe Tunnel in its stride. 10 June 1967.

I'm fond of this picture because, for me, it captures a sense of space and freedom enjoyed in those chalk hills south of Dorchester. Here Merchant Navy Pacific No 35023 *Holland-Afrika* Line speeds a Waterloo-bound train down the 1 in 91 gradient from Bincombe Tunnel. 10 June 1967.

A splendid sight – immaculate Merchant Navy Class Pacific No 35028 *Clan Line*, assisted by a diesel banking at the rear, lifts its Weymouth-Waterloo boat train towards the summit at Bincombe Tunnel. 10 June 1967.

Bathed in glorious sunshine, Merchant Navy Pacific No 35030 *Elder Dempster Lines* heads for the hills, after which the fireman can relax during the easy descent to Weymouth. Originally constructed during World War ll, Merchant Navy Class locomotives were named after the shipping lines involved in the Battle of the Atlantic. The last were built in 1949 and named after the shipping lines that used the docks the Southern Railway served. 10 June 1967.

Hauling a parcels train, Merchant Navy Pacific No 35008 *Orient Line* plods up the steeply graded 1 in 50 line to the quaintly named Upwey Wishing Well Halt before plunging into the first of the two Bincombe Tunnels at the summit, between Weymouth and Dorchester. The halt was so named because George III drank from the wishing well using a gold cup. It was opened and closed on the same dates as Monkton and Came Halt, north of the twin tunnels. 10 June 1967.

This page and opposite: Working hard, and having just burst out of the shorter of the two Bincombe Tunnels before plunging into the next, West Country Pacific No 34100 *Appledore* is assisted on the climb by a 'Crompton' diesel pilot. The attractive grasses embellish the lineside in the early evening sun. 10 June 1967.

An impressive pairing of un-rebuilt and rebuilt West Country Pacifics. No 34023 *Blackmore Vale* leads No 34108 *Wincanton* as this brace of Bulleids slow to a stop to pick up some enthusiasts at Radipole Halt. We are then treated to a splendid percussive departure, as they attack the 1 in 74 gradient, steepening to 1 in 50, towards the summit. By 1961, out of a class of 110 Light Pacifics, 60 had been rebuilt into what looked like totally different engines. Ironically, at 90 tons, four tons heavier than the un-rebuilds, weight precluded these locomotives from a number of secondary routes in the South West. 18 June 1967.

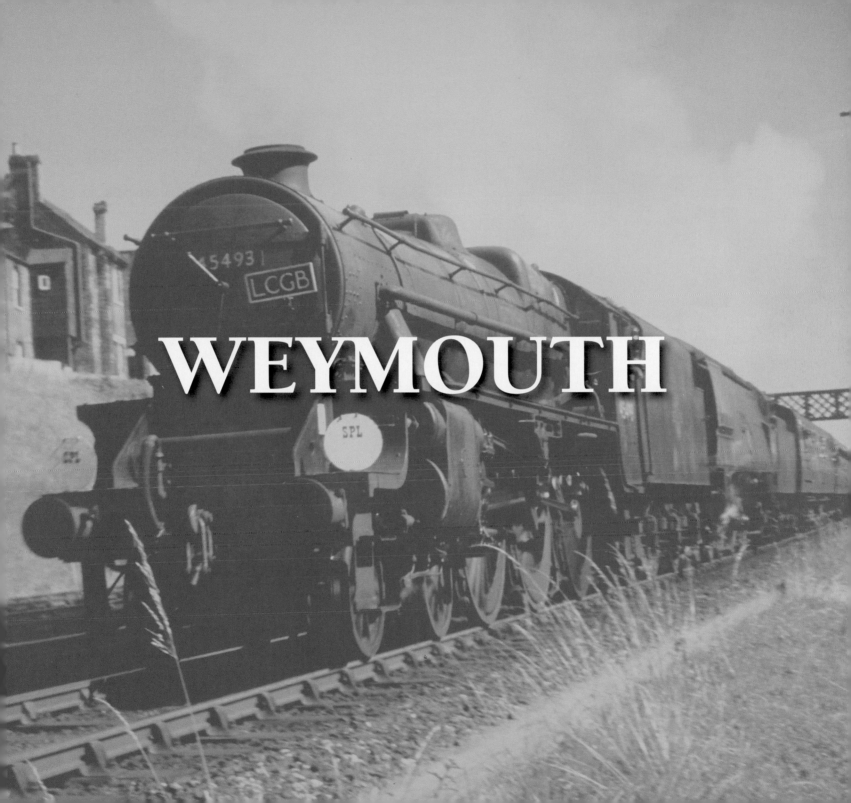

WEYMOUTH

Preserved ex-LNER A4 Class Pacific No 4498 *Sir Nigel Gresley* brings a 'streak' to the Southern. The streamlined loco-motive, in impressive LNER garter blue livery, passes disused Monkton and Came Halt with an enthusiasts' special for Weymouth. 4 June 1967.

Preparing for the homeward run. LNER A4 Pacific No4498 *Sir Nigel Gresley* is turned, coaled and watered at Weymouth motive power depot. 4 June 1967.

A special visitor from the north was ex-LNER A4 Pacific No 60024 *Kingfisher*. Unlike *Sir Nigel Gresley*, which was preserved, *Kingfisher* was still in active service with BR and was normally based at Aberdeen. It had travelled south to work an enthusiasts' special to Weymouth, and another the following day to Exeter. 26 March 1967.

While the Southern had its streamlined or un-rebuilt Light Pacifics ('air smoothed' according to their designer OVS Bulleid), the LNER had its graceful A4s or 'streaks' as they were known. Here, No 60024 *Kingfisher* catches a welcome burst of sun on a showery day as it leaves Weymouth. 26 March 1967.

This page and opposite: Stanier Black Five 4-6-0 No 45493 pilots West Country Class Pacific No 34100 *Appledore* towards Weymouth with a railtour which included a trip along Weymouth Quay tramway. As I swung around to grab another shot the sun glinted off the burnished copper piping of this immaculately polished locomotive. Note the knotted hanky. Very seaside! 3 July 1966.

This page and opposite: The ex-LMS Black Five No 45493 and West Country No 34100 *Appledore* have uncoupled from their train and pulled forward to allow Ivatt 2MT 2-6-2T No 41298 to take the railtour along the Weymouth Quay branch. The last steam locomotive to do so. 3 July 1966.

A bustle of bystanders, photographers and railwaymen… Pedestrians watch this unexpected entertainment unfold as No 41298 makes cautious progress along the quay tramway. Photographers jockey for good positions, while a pair of flagmen walk ahead of the train. In its heyday this line was frequented by boat trains conveying passengers and van trains transporting produce such as tomatoes and broccoli, from the Channel Islands. Scheduled services ceased in 1987. 3 July 1966.

Immaculately turned out, Ivatt 2MT No 41298 holds up the traffic as it hauls its train, at walking pace, towards Weymouth Quay. 3 July 1966.

This page and opposite: Ready to play its part in the return run of the railtour is un-rebuilt West Country Pacific No 34002 *Salisbury* seen being coaled and watered at Weymouth sheds. Salisbury gained fame for hauling the last steam train from Plymouth to Penzance and back in 1964. Nice for Southern enthusiasts, but maybe it rancoured with die-hard GWR fans possibly anticipating something more Western to sign off steam in Cornwall. Oh well, a point to the Southern in the old regional rivalry pay-back stakes. 3 July 1966.

Having been turned and prepared for the road, Black Five 4-6-0 No 45493 blows off steam, while in the background West Country *Appledore* reverses out towards the main line. There almost seemed to be an 'open day' atmosphere at Weymouth motive power depot on this occasion, as virtually everyone who was on the special seemed to be wandering around the sheds! 3 July 1966.

Building up speed for the climb ahead, Black Five No 45493 and West Country Class *Salisbury* accelerate away from Weymouth. 3 July 1966.

My first photograph of main line steam at Weymouth was BR Standard Class 5 4-6-0 No 73114 *Etarre* departing with a passenger train. A total of 172 were built, and 20 of the Southern Region locomotives were named after SR King Arthur Class locomotives that were then being withdrawn. October 1965.

Heading for Bournemouth and beyond… Two BR Standard Class 5 4-6-0s prepared to depart with the 11.18 from Weymouth. The train engine is No 73029 and the pilot engine, which came off at Dorchester, is No 73002. 10 December 1966.

Ex-LMS Ivatt 2-6-2T No 41298 is acting station pilot and shunting coaches and forming trains at Weymouth station. 30 April 1966.

Racing down the final gradient on the approach to Weymouth, and leaving a threatening sky behind, is BR Standard Class 4 4-6-0 No 75079. 26 March 1966.

This page and opposite: A treat, in a time of rapidly diminishing un-rebuilt Bulleid Light Pacifics, was the arrival of Battle of Britain Class No 34064 *Fighter Command*. This locomotive was the only member of its class to be fitted with a Giesel ejector, a specially-designed blast-pipe to reduce coal consumption. British Railways only fitted it to one other locomotive, a BR Standard Class 9F 2-10-0. Having been released from its train, *Fighter Command* then backed down towards the sheds. Sadly, it was withdrawn the month after this picture was taken. 30 April 1966.

Rebuilt Battle of Britain Class Pacific No 34077 *603 Squadron* temporarily blots out the sun with an eruption of smoke as it pulls away from Weymouth station. This class was named after aircraft, airfields, squadrons and personalities of the Battle of Britain when Britain stood alone against the enemy, defended by the brave men and women of the RAF. 30 April 1966.

Ivatt 2MT 2-6-2T No 41301 shunts empty coaching stock at Weymouth. Although their origins are in the LMS many Ivatt tanks migrated to the Southern Region, and gave good service on mixed duties. They became so much a part of the regional scene it became hard to think of them as anything but Southern! 3 July 1966.

A wailing whistle heralded the departure of BR Standard Class 5 4-6-0 No 73155 with the 16.47 for Bournemouth. 30 April 1966.

Above left: Merchant Navy Class Pacific No 35008 *Orient Line* piles on the power as it gets into its stride with a Weymouth departure. 30 April 1966.

Above right: Journey's end for BR Class 4 2-6-0 No 76058 as it stops just short of the buffers at Weymouth. It is interesting to note the Royal Mail coaches in green livery. This travelling Post Office operated between Weymouth and Waterloo and ceased in 1988. 30 April 1966.

Even begrimed with dirt, the West Countries potently evoke visions of their namesakes. Urban dwellers might find a name like *Dartmoor* conjures images of purple heather and gorse-clad slopes crowned with rugged, granite tors. Then again they might not, and simply visualise swirling mist, the hairy hand and escaped prisoners! 26 March 1966.

It took a lot of coal to fuel a fleet of steam locomotives in a shed with the capacity of Weymouth. Here can be seen the sidings for coal wagons, positioned beside the elevated coal stage. 30 April 1966.

West Country Pacific No 34095 *Brentor* looks serene as it simmers in early evening sunlight. All locomotives, on arrival at the locomotive power depot, were turned in readiness for their next duty – which inevitably meant facing north. It is a chance to reflect on those instantly recognisable characteristics of a Bulleid Pacific be it "air smoothed" or rebuilt. 10 June 1967.

Also that evening Merchant Navy Class Pacific No 35003 *Royal Mail* was in light steam. 10 June 1967.

I think this has to be my all time favourite. It is that Radio 4 Desert Island Discs moment – the one luxury item ("…apart from the Bible and Shakespeare!") you can take while marooned on your remote island. This image somehow distills all that heady atmosphere of a main line steamshed. Framed from the dark cool of within, a trio of Bulleid Pacifics – No 34047 *Callington*, No 34077 *603 Squadron* and No 34008 *Padstow*, bask in the sun on a particularly balmy April afternoon. 30 April 1966.

At over 69 ft long, 2 ft longer than the Bulleid Light Pacifics, the Battle of Britain and West Country Classes, Merchant Navy Class Pacific No 35030 *Elder Dempster Lines* only just fits on to the turntable. There is not a lot of room to manoeuvre All locomotives had to be turned using manpower to push the turntable around. Note the cast iron sign that says: ALL ENGINES must STOP before going on this TURNTABLE. 30 April 1966.

Complete with its nameplate, Battle of Britain Pacific No 34089 *602 Squadron* awaits its next duty. The term "Pacific" referred to the wheel arrangement which was 4-6-2. 26 March 1966.

A general view of the locomotive sidings with Ivatt 2MT 2-6-2T No 41298, and BR Standard Class 5 No 73080 *Merlin* a number of Bulleid Pacifics and a 'Crompton' D6504. 26 March 1966.

BR Standard Class 5 4-6-0 No 73018 and Ivatt tank No 41301 seen on my first visit to Weymouth. Autumn, 1965.

Having hauled a train into Weymouth, West Country Class Pacific No 34008 Padstow reverses back towards the sheds. The two lines nearest the camera were used for locomotive movements. 30 April 1966.

BR Standard Class 4 2-6-0 No 76013 reverses through the shed roads on its way to the turntable. 26 March 1966.

A powerhouse of Bulleid Pacifics. In the foreground is Merchant Navy No 35007 *Aberdeen Commonwealth*, to the left West Country Class No 34093 *Saunton* and, centre, is sister locomotive No 34021 *Dartmoor*. 2 July 1967.

This page and opposite: It is eight days before electrification of the Waterloo-Bournemouth line and the end of Southern steam. That end came a week early for me because, on that fateful day, we were due to head off on the annual family holiday! My last visit was to see Merchant Navy Pacific No 35008 Orient Line on a trip organised by the Southern Region to mark the end of steam. No 35008 was superbly turned out and had been reunited with its nameplate for the occasion. At Weymouth motive power depot the Merchant Navy Pacific is being coaled. It is a handsomely turned out representative of a class of 30 locomotives that had, down the years, put in sterling service on the Waterloo-Weymouth, Waterloo-Exeter main lines. In the background the new order, a Brush Type 4 diesel leaves Weymouth with an up passenger train. 2 July 1967.

Merchant Navy No 35007 *Aberdeen Commonwealth*, minus nameplates, pilots the next numerical member of the class, No 35008 *Orient Line*, as they dig into the climb out of Weymouth with the returning railtour. 2 July 1967.

Shortly after the departure of the double-headed Merchant Navy-hauled special, West Country No 34021 *Dartmoor* backed down to the station yard. It then hauled a goods train to the foot of the initial 1 in 187 incline. Here, No 34093 *Saunton* attached itself to the rear and the pair blasted their way out of Weymouth. *Saunton* acted as a banker for the climb that would steepen from 1 in 74 to 1 in 50 and finally 1 in 52 before peaking at Bincombe Tunnel.

Appropriately the departing shot of *Saunton*, my favorite class of locomotive, made a fitting last image in quest to photograph steam on the Southern. I like to think those boys, clearly enthralled by the passing spectacle of such might, took away some of the magic, the way I did when I was their age... 2 July 1967.

144

Appropriately the departing shot of *Saunton*, my favorite class of locomotive, made a fitting last image in quest to photograph steam on the Southern. I like to think those boys, clearly enthralled by the passing spectacle of such might, took away some of the magic, the way I did when I was their age... 2 July 1967.

Shortly after the departure of the double-headed Merchant Navy-hauled special, West Country No 34021 *Dartmoor* backed down to the station yard. It then hauled a goods train to the foot of the initial 1 in 187 incline. Here, No 34093 *Saunton* attached itself to the rear and the pair blasted their way out of Weymouth. *Saunton* acted as a banker for the climb that would steepen from 1 in 74 to 1 in 50 and finally 1 in 52 before peaking at Bincombe Tunnel.